Love
is a song she sang from a cage

Bianca Bowers

Love is a song she sang from a Cage
COPYRIGHT © 2016 BIANCA BOWERS
Published by Paperfields Press

Book Cover Art
Woman's face © Anna Ismagilova, Shutterstock 1501996802
Background © Art Furnace, Shutterstock 1214207470

Book Cover Design by Bianca Bowers
Interior Art © Shutterstock 146456681 / 230326585 / 11786773 / 123544597

All rights reserved. No part of this publication may be reproduced, distributed, or transmitted in any form or by any means, including photocopying, recording, or other electronic or mechanical methods, without the prior written permission of the publisher, except in the case of brief quotations embodied in critical reviews and certain other noncommercial uses permitted by copyright law. For permission requests, email the publisher: "Attention: Permissions"
info@paperfieldspress.com
www.paperfieldspress.com

Paperback ISBN-13: 978-0-6484426-3-9
Hardcover ISBN-13: 978-0-9942404-4-6
EPub ISBN-13: 978-0-9942404-6-0

This edition, January 2020

Books by Bianca Bowers

Cape of Storms (Auteur Books, 2019)
Butterfly Voyage (Paperfields Press, 2018)
Pressed Flowers (Paperfields Press, 2017)
Love is a song she sang from a cage (Paperfields Press, 2016)
Passage (Paperfields Press, 2015)
Death and Life (Paperfields Press, 2014)

For

L'oisseau chanteur

To

Sa liberté

Poems

Caged

Love is a Song	3
City	5
Hummingbird Heart	7
Branches	9
Constant Cravings	10
Sliver	11
Casablanca	12
Seasons	13
Breakage	14
Venus	15
Fingerprints	16
Emptied	17
Fight for love	18

Feathers

Freefall	21
Upended	22
Mermaid	23
Appetite	25
Hungry	27
Solstice	28
Reincarnation	32

Without You	33
Island	36

Songbird

Chemistry	39
Tequila	41
Arithmetic	42
Jet lagged	43
Between Literary Heart Beats	44
Shakespeare	46
Haemorrhage	47
Timer	48
Flammable	49
Suicidal Heart	50
Fortune's Widow	52
Kiss of Death	54
Edit	55
Impact	56

Flight

Distance	59
Metaphors	60
Exile	61
Hemisphere	62
Titanic	63
Death and Life	64

Remains	65
Premonition	66
Indigo Arch	67
Fate	68
Je Ne Regrette Rien	69
Shipwrecked	70
Liberté	71
Ego	72
Manuscript	73
Nothing	74
Genesis	76
Love Paradigm	78
Afterword	81
About the Author	83

Caged

Love is a song

Love is a song
she sang from a cage

Her mahogany eyes cast expressionist shadows
that drew me into her noir mise en scène
where her voice lingered like a spirit in purgatory
where she sang her songs, a book of stories burdened
with blue,
night after night.

I kissed her pomegranate lips,
hummed her vintage tune
      until it rattled the ribs of my soul.

I stroked her feathery fingers,
      let her strum my acoustic heart strings.

I sipped her voice
      until I changed colour,
          like a thousand raindrops on copper.

Her darkness was a bulb that lit the room,
and I chain-smoked her sadness like the menthol
cigarettes I snuck at sixteen.

She was a songbird in a world of noise,
a bruise of a girl in a world of collisions,
a silhouette in the ether.

I longed to be those wounded words
that sibilated on her tongue
that entered the raw atmosphere, like newborns.
I longed to catch them, like butterflies in a net,
to nurse them back to health,
for they were as tender as those secrets
hidden in my deepest pockets.

I made love to her like a spirit without a body,
cradled her like a wounded sparrow,
drank her tears like bourbon.

I slept inside the universal truth of her song,
willed the music to haunt my dreams at night,

and, when I woke
I was floating above love, looking down at it,
like a bird
freed from its cage.

City

I hid a city
beneath my skin
grew dandelions in my head

so I could blow those wispy sails
like kisses,
wishes on the wind,

willing you to hear the voices calling you
closer to my church
to climb under my fate

share my pulse
love me between the shadows
until we eclipsed.

You always had me
at the edge of myself;
a hibiscus trellis

suspended
above brambles
the wind our only accompaniment

scattering seeds
far far
out of reach

travelling in perpetuity
between stars, between seasons
Our hearts beating
on the horizon.

Hummingbird Heart

Clumps of words
line my throat
      like iridescent feathers
but they cannot escape
must remain
silent
says the cage
says the songbird

This song in my heart
cannot be released
for its lyrics
could strip the gold lacquer
adorning my aviary

So I write

I write this music
that has no voice
across my chest
my lips
my breasts
wanting him to read them
in his dreams

So I write

I write these lyrics
that cannot be sung
cannot be carried
by the breath of my lungs
lest they explode
like diesel, kerosine, gasoline - lit

So I write

These words
that cannot be justified
cannot be altered
in meaning
cannot be scribbled over
lest they kill the chorus
of my heart
my hummingbird heart
that was born to sing

Branches

You flicker in front of me
A black and white movie

I dream in circles
kiss a phantom
Choke on the vapour of texts

It can never be enough
to live inside a book
Romance needs oxygen
like fire

And although this fire has been lit
it cannot burn without a body

And I wonder about past lives
If we've met and loved before

For flowers cannot grow without stalks
Yet here I am
preparing the branches in my heart
for Spring

Constant Cravings

You make me want to read. To gorge on words like a starving book worm, or a down and out poet.

You make me want. What I can't have. But I have tasted your words, and now it's constant cravings.

Sliver

I am happy. Content with what I've got. With where I am. Sort of. Mostly.

If I was the moon, I would be a sliver away from full. One shade away from blood.

Casablanca

We kissed
like Bergman and Bogart
a plane hangar between us

Je t'aime
I whispered
but the wind
stole my words
before they found your ear

and though we embraced like lovers
from another lifetime

it was the last kiss
in Casablanca.

Seasons

I have never excelled with this tree called Love

Only climbed, caressed and fallen from
its branches,

but

like a newly planted sapling in Winter
- dead within the first week -
Love has been seasons
out of sync.

Breakage

I won't deny my heart

My head, maybe

who only understands
halves and breakage

who is trained in politics
and corruption
assassination and lies

but knows nothing of arts
and culture.

Venus

Excuse Venus
while she stores her dreams
beneath a star

Excuse her til then

if then breathes
        inside a constellation
if then is more tangible
than a word -
        a partition
shield
        defence.

You don't think love is
enough
but it's the closest planet
in our solar system

Fingerprints

I am overcome
by this distance
between our skin

the proximity of my heart
to yours
is crushing

and yet

I haven't touched your face
or smelt your cologne

and yet

this exquisite intimacy
this staggering isolation

has the fingerprints of decades

Emptied

I love you
I miss you

I have emptied these words
of meaning

what started as a bookend
for impossible mileage
is hollow and crestfallen
can bring no relief
no satisfaction

                for you are there
                in the sky
and I am here
in my cage

light years from freedom.

Fight for love

I never thought
to fight for love
after walking away,
disgraced.

I never wanted
to fight for love
until now.

Feathers

Freefall

Reckless
while the moon gathers blood
while my heart is on loan

Restless
to strike that match
while my belly churns
tinder

Beseeching
resurrection
as we freefall
into love.

Upended

I love you
seems so insubstantial
for this cyclone of emotions
that sweep
and consume me

I am the oak tree
upended
the bird fallen
from its nest

and while I don't know
what this is, exactly
I do know
that I love you
is not enough.

Mermaid

You have unleashed a storm
this rain will never stop
it seems
and it has been so long with sunshine
that I don't care

Let that rain pour
torrential
thunder stamping
lightning crackling
Deluge
debauchery
drowning

I want to drown;
Suicidal for a mortal
Salvation for a mermaid

You have given me scales
my love
liberated my very breath
so that I am at home in the ocean
again

I watch the tides gather

like overhanging storm clouds

reaching hysterical crescendo

where stars align

where planets eclipse

where I see the sky

and realise it is not blue

but something else entirely

- a transparent lake edged with silver stars -

Appetite

I cannot eat
cannot sleep
with and without you
I am fucked
fated
foreign

My appetite rages
but not for food
so my weight whittles
I turn nymph-like
like a water sprite
except there is no water in sight
and I am thirsty
so thirsty
my love

Let me drink
let me eat
what I crave
before I wither and die
in this famine
this war of the heart

Let me go
and take me back
turn yourself inside out
for me
because I ask you
for this is what love is

irrational
lawless
irreverent

Be irreverent with me
love
Be faithless
for love
unfaithful
for faith

Let me go
or I may never
return.

Hungry

I am Catherine Tramell
hungry to write,
fucking experience
like an insatiable lover

I set myself alight
so I can burn
feel the sensation
reach hysterical blindness.

Solstice

I'm writing again
because of you

because you saw me
when I couldn't see myself

and I love you
like my copy of Wuthering Heights
so tattered and torn
a cherished heirloom of literature

But oh how my heart sobs over this mileage
that separates
Cathy from her Heathcliff

Fill my head
with question marks
while I write love poems
for a fictional lover
while I dream of us
reading, laughing, talking
beyond twilight
Your velvet voice
reading an entire library

nights, mornings, days
filled
with intoxicating words
this shared language
this magic and mystery
that flickers like a fairy's wand

Let me dream
before these moth wings
disintegrate in morning dew

Ask me that question
that hopeless question
before we say goodbye

Goodbye
the only thing I hate about you,
when you abandon me
in those hours of silence
Lovers' hours
that tick between tidal clocks
indifferently
cruelly
selfishly

And although you try to reassure me
by omitting that word
goodbye
Goodbye it is as Shakespeare well knew
Parting is such sweet sorrow
when the sweetness sours
and the sorrow sinks like solstice

My initial hope
that bird of infinite possibility
that flapped its wings
when my heart woke at sunrise
is flying overhead
so high, I cannot reach it
feet buried
eyes in heaven
watching it fly over
like a jet plane
I have missed

And I want to weep
want to write science fiction
and time travel to you

But we may never be

my love...

a night emptied of stars
a moon without rocks
an ocean without tides
a death without a body

Reincarnation

Cruel love, I didn't ask
for a funeral in the rain
I am strong
but not invincible
Don't reincarnate yourself like this, love
love
love...

Without You

Today, I am exiguous
I am semi-circles
and sickle moons
Upside down, without you.

Craving proximity
intimacy with love
the kind that turns water into wine
sex into love
atoms into molecules

Today, my wings are horns
and Lucifer is closer than God
That picture of you, that I keep
is not enough
of a substitute
for your lips
bruising skin,
your gaze reflecting,
      your words in my mouth.

Today, I am fire
at its most vicious
White hot love

straight from the furnace
You can't touch me
hell, I can't touch me
I've moved beyond colour
into shades of ghost

I am lost
I am found
    I will never find my way back
and simultaneously home
    in your eyes
    in the jagged creases of your words
    where you rock my heart in your palm

Today, I am here
I am there
everywhere
nowhere
Circling the globe
like a lovesick nomad
I am fear
I am not afraid
of you
of me
of us

Petals so red
they saturate my blood
with courage
Imbibe me
put a wreath around my neck
take me to an island
and fuck me
until this madness runs clear

Because today
I am exiguous
Scissored sunshine
orphaned rainbow
cosmic confusion
without you.

Island

I'm on an island
love
dreaming a while

Me and you
the hands on our wrists
in sync

Tracing your lips with a
look
loving you under the moonlight

I'm on an island tonight
love
dream with me

Songbird

Chemistry

Life dilates
                du coeur
cannot steady
or disengage

This humming and hissing
of wires
destined to spark
fated to burn

Own the madness, I say
fuck or abstain
there's not a damn bit of difference
nothing
will reverse this chemistry

So leave me be
and let me burn
burn
burn
at your feet
in your palms
against your skin
on your tongue

Because without this
we are Poets without pens
Lovers
without chemistry

Tequila

I taunt myself
with your beautiful face

Taste those thousand
million miles between us
like a shot of tequila

They tell lies;
absence is the antithesis
of fondness
and my heart is jet lagged
from travelling
all the way
across
that bleeding ocean.

Arithmetic

We are caricatures;
Adam and Eve
a red apple between us
pierced with a medieval arrow
cupid's fingerprints all over it

So we tie our heads together
trace our tongues around solutions
that neither can swallow
play ring-a-rosies with time

For our hearts, who are lovers
in spite of arithmetic.

Jet Lagged

I can see my ribs
in your reflection

In just three days
they're as vulnerable
as my heart

but I am not jet lagged
anymore

we exchange sunrise
and sunset
moon and sun

so we can love
for now
at least

Between Literary Heart Beats

I sit at a writing desk
surrounded by art nouveau
and poetry books

Between literary heart beats

I turn on the tv
only to find lovers
staring back at me
taunting with their nakedness
their unrestricted passion
their fictional perfection

Between literary heart beats

I sit cross-legged
with my dreams and desires
so misplaced
so misguided
so out of sync with fate
and fortune
and I wonder why
these triangles cannot be circles

Between literary heart beats
I sip tea and daydream
about reading Eliot
sharing coffee and teaspoons
with you
leaving my fingerprints
on your copy of Prufrock

Between literary heart beats

Shakespeare

You make me want to quote Shakespeare. Goddamned Shakespeare. Whom I rejected, once my heart abandoned the romance of architecture and began climbing skyscrapers.

I think of Romeo and Juliette. Anthony and Cleopatra. Those epic, fated, tragic lovers that drank from love's cup but once. I think of Cleopatra's monologue:

> oh happy horse to bear the weight of Anthony

The burden of love still light on her tongue.

Only, I am no Cleopatra. I am Juliette with her teenage desire; ambivalent about poison and war.

Oh, Shakespeare. Why fill my head with tales, lines, history, tragedy, melodrama? I exiled you to the shelf for good reason, and now I cannot help but cradle your spine in my palms and drink your words like they are my last supper.

Haemorrhage

The hairline cracks deepen
my love
Your heart slips away
Your gaze flickers
like a paraffin lamp in a blackout

I haemorrhage love at your feet
but you don't look down
from your halo of smoke rings

Timer

I cannot expect you to accept this
bomb
that will detonate
one way or another

perhaps it's too late already
the timer is set
the wires are hissing
and my heart is remote controlled

Flammable

I am strong, fierce, fearless
But I cannot survive

if this emotion is as flammable
as I suspect it is

Once we strike the match
our fire will burn the house down
taking everyone in it

If we are fated to burn
we will reduce everything else to ash

Suicidal Heart

My heart skips beats like a stylus on vinyl
it catches and trips on the parallel grooves
of a life
out of reach
        the one where I'm scratched
        bygone
        tangled inside
        music and melody

My heart spins and burns
like a catherine wheel on guy fawkes
ignites between parallel seams
of a life
in smouldering ruins
        lighting fluid in a palm of tinder
        burning like an effigy
        caught
        between ignition and explosion

My heart is suicidal, a girl on a bridge
haemorrhaging love
like the river swelling beneath her feet
suspended
between oceans

shipwrecked
        unseasonably buried
        adrift
        between deep water and shore

My heart is trapped in a gilded cage
yearning for flight
perched alongside a window
with a view of sky and wings
and all I can do is imagine
life abroad
        the one where I'm a songbird
        the one where I sing
        the one where I'm caught
                between freedom and
forever

Fortune's Widow

You were right
love
this is crazy
illogical
irrational
fated
fortune's widow

We cannot close
circles with squares
cannot row without oars
fly without wings

It is all so faded
now
scorched by the sun
of reality

Spring and Autumn
will never be the same
after this Winter, this Summer
of longing
dreaming
imagining

of electricity

and snow storms

Kiss of Death

I cannot survive this
simultaneous flood and drought
where my heart is a row boat
and a flower

Edit

I cannot live two lives
at once
one will destroy the other
like the darlings in my stories
they cannot all survive

and while it pains me to edit
my heart
I know I must

Impact

Stay there love
in the belly of the moon

for you are mortal
cannot breathe
underwater.

for it is impossible
to survive
this impact

only scavengers
will search
the detritus

Stay there love
and save yourself
from me.

Flight

Distance

The distance grows
impossibly

I cannot communicate
in monosyllables anymore

I would not love the ocean
if she were shallow
and I cannot love you
like this

So I will stop
like a hurricane before its death

Shut this silliness
like the last page of a book
the ending no longer a mystery

Metaphors

These metaphors drive me crazy
when I want reality

My imagination, no comfort
when I crave tangibles

Your adjectives, not enough
when I need verbs

Together, impossible
as long as our love is limited
to poetry

Exile

You make me want to crank the volume
and mute it simultaneously
but I am not an in-between girl
Give me the noise
or exile me to silence

Do not whisper and shout
when it suits you
I want it all
or I will choose nothing

Hemisphere

I cannot trust the voices
inside my head
when I emerge at sunrise
and you disappear
into twilight

I cannot live in this
split hemisphere
disjointed seasons
where nothing can grow

I cannot breathe
when you withhold words
the things I love most

our heartbeat, I would argue

When you leave me
like this
slip between timezones
I obsess

Titanic

It is late
on the Eastern seaboard
The coast is silent
between us

Silent enough to drown
in slipstreams of doubt
and logic

When you are not here
you are missed
I am lonely
without you

I know
that we cannot continue
like lovers
aboard the Titanic

because we both need
magic
and dragonflies
to keep this afloat

Death and Life

You have liberated me love
ruined me
Our breaths have merged
and I gasp between goodbyes

I have been up since 3 am
scheming in every language
and I am breathless now
running and running
toward you
away from you

I have written my shoulders
into figures of eight
tensed fingers at the thought
that this feeling will end
that this force will die
before we get a chance to nurture it

My love
my love

This is death and life
all over again

Remains

Inevitable decay begins
A heart drowning
in its own amniotic fluid

Yet I cannot bare to bury our love
nor cremate our love poems
and scatter them for the crows

Premonition

It's time to say goodbye

    the plane hangar

    my Casablanca dream

    was a premonition
    after all.

Indigo Arch

You told me
you were not afraid
yet here you are
silent for days
withholding love

While my heart withers
like a sunburnt lawn
and shrinks like a dehydrated river

Still, I won't reject this karma
For your love has transplanted my lungs
like a charitable donor

How can I blame the volatile sky
for offering an indigo arch?

Fate

I miss you
like I miss the sun
in Winter

Slow and torturous
A memory erased

And the worst part of this death
is knowing how it cradled me
before I lost it

All thanks to
some goddamned fate
or human bullshit
or worse
My own making

Je Ne Regrette Rien

The songbird has sung
escaped her gilded cage
and he is not there
to meet her in the sky
never was
it was all a figment
of a too-small heart, made big
compounded words
making up for lost time
and all she can think to say is

Je Ne Regrette Rien.

Shipwrecked

Rain in reverse
we are

Shiny bright things
we were

While summer raged
in our shipwrecked
hearts

Liberté

I sleep steeped in moonlight
And breathe in dust
A Chimera takes flight
in my caliginous sky
Athena rests
in delta sleep
Ma liberté est arrivé

Ego

My heart is naive
again
after decades of realism
Young again,
wistful
and pure
in its desire
an ego without an id.

Manuscript

A handwritten manuscript
remains
but the plot is
unreliable

I think of you
more than I should

Nothing

The sky sets before the sun
My head is a book of poems
My hummingbird heart is free

I wait
in the lavender groves
for your return
from the Full Moon Hotel

           but grow restless
       when I think of us

So I carry hibiscus sandals in one hand
and twirl bramble hair with the other
until I reach the end of the pier
to watch the blue jellyfish bloom

We have kissed without kissing
made love without a bed
mapped tattoos without ink

Your hands are black
and mine are red
but love keeps us colour blind

buries any crimes
we may have committed

And I wait,
inside my solar clocktower
like the moon waits for the sun
to sink

and I promise to wait forever-
                until guns stop firing
                until humans stop hurting

      for there is nothing

           nothing
that will keep me
from you

not even you.

Genesis

I'm a girl on a cornish cliff
with arms outstretched
with empty hands

and the ocean overflows
with anger
from the stormy night
that still hangs in the sky

and my heart has been
emptied
of swells
replaced with rocks
salty grief
that stings my blue eyes

as much as yesterday's rejection
when you abandoned ship
and decommissioned the lighthouse
that rescued us

and the angry waves
amplify
into ungovernable tears

launching my heart into freefall
from that craggy ledge
down
down
down

until I plunge into ocean
arms
permit myself to feel it all
unedited, for once

until the salt dehydrates
the rocks retreat into sea foam
and I see my empty hands
for what they really are

Open palms;
receivers
for genesis.

Love Paradigm

Where does love come from?
Where does it go?

That crackling birth
and monotone death

Are we nothing more than
lithium-
batteries
with an expiration

And if this is true
then we misunderstand
love

for it shouldn't be imprisoned
obsessed over, smothered, possessed
does not belong to us

love has a birthday and a death
an inevitable denouement
after a glorious climax

destined for reincarnation

Perhaps it's our thoughts
about love
that cause its downfall

> we think too little
> and feel too much
> in the beginning

> think too much
> and feel too little
> in the end

What if our brains are slaveowners
and love was never meant to be imprisoned?

Afterword

This is a special and unique book for me because it wasn't planned but rather gifted to me from some other plane. I literally wrote it over a 12-hour period, between the hours of 1am and 1pm, after waking up with a feverish mind. The writing process was trance-like, and unlike any of my other books, which I write, edit, and revise innumerable times before they're ready to publish. *Love is a song she sang from a cage* was published a month after I wrote it—and most of that time was spent on cover design and typesetting.

      It is also unfamiliar and uncomfortable territory for me—a book of passionate love poems—a genre I don't usually read, write, or particularly enjoy. Which perhaps explains why these poems were channelled and not planned—a subconscious response to an intense emotional experience that I had no idea how to articulate at the time.

      At its core, that unarticulated experience was the one-love-til-death-do-us-part ideology. By nature, a long-term union is demanding and punctuated with compromise. But at what personal cost? If the needs of the union are always placed above the needs of the individuals, then isn't it more of a dictatorship than a democracy?

This revolutionary idea of dictatorship versus democracy became the seed of my second novel, *Three Hearts*, which I am revising and editing as I write this in January 2020 and is due to be published in late 2020 by Auteur Books.

About the Author

Bianca Bowers is a South African-born, Australian-based writer who has also lived in the UK and New Zealand. She holds a BA in English and Film/TV/Media Studies and her poems have appeared in film, print anthologies, and online journals over the last twenty years.

Bianca is the author of *Cape of Storms*, as well as five poetry books. Her second novel, *Three Hearts*, is due in 2020.

You can find her at:
www.biancabowers.com

To leave a review, please visit:
https://amazon.com/author/biancabowers
https://www.goodreads.com/BiancaBowersAuthor

www.ingramcontent.com/pod-product-compliance
Lightning Source LLC
Chambersburg PA
CBHW032046290426
44110CB00012B/976